MINDFUL MOTION

OCEAN IN THE DROP

TRESH AN L.

CW01497170

MINDFUL MOTION

OCEAN IN THE DROP

First Edition

DEDICATION

To those who have walked by me side by side, through
the good and rough, you are beacons of light.

Other Books by Tresh An:

Mindful Motion: 33 Flames of Burning Desire

Contents

Preface

You are not just a drop in the ocean,
you are the mighty ocean in the drop.

-RUMI

Everyone has their take and understanding of wholeness or oneness, as others would call it. For the more scientifically inclined, this could well be the study of fractals. Though, what is it to be the ocean in the drop? The opening metaphor by Sufi poet Rumi is a poignant one. He uses the symbol of water to show that everything around us and in us is all one thing and contained inside tiny fragment or in the case of the metaphor one tiny droplet.

Bob Marley shared his thoughts on water, where he used rain as an example, showing what effect water has on different psyches:

Some people feel the rain, some people just get wet.

Da Vinci said water was a conductor of all things natural:

Water is the driving force of all nature.

Bruce Lee conveyed his thoughts on the oneness or totality of water:

Water can flow or crash, be water my friend.

In 2010, I laid there motionless, looking up at the sky, closing my eyes, looking back up at the sky, not saying a word. I narrowly escaped a fatal situation, which I was lucky enough not to need the hospital for. Since then I have made it my commitment to honour the flow of life. Something pushed me to start writing poetry after that day.

I am intrigued by the manner in which poetry is never quite finished. As the iconic inventor and sculptor said, art is never finished, only abandoned. In terms of writing, some poems seem to flow easy to me, whereas others take a lifetime of experience to write up. Whether or not it takes a long time to write or not, poetry to me represents movement.

A year later in 2011, I came up with the concept of initially doing one Mindful Motion book. This was later split into two books, this one being Ocean In The Drop, the poem book and the other, 33 Flames of Burning Desire a guided mediation which reads more like collected essays. Is that the only difference between the two?

For starters this one is a symbol of water and totality. The other is a symbol of fire and individuality. The two books represent dichotomies. Also, unlike its more narrative centric counterpart 33 Flames of Burning Desire, this book is comprised entirely of poetry.

Author's Note

The urge to put pen to paper and write some poetry arose a few days before my birthday in 2010. Though I am young(ish) at the time of writing this now, I was barely out of my teenage years when I faced what I described in the preface. Firstly, I realised how precious and valuable time is. Secondly I needed a vice to channel my energies into something productive and useful; ergo, in my world, poetry became celebrated and appreciated.

The beauty of poetry is that it can affect different people on different levels. The best poems are simple and have to be read multiple times to derive more meaning from it. Other poems are straightforward and metaphorically hit you in the face from the first impression.

In terms of marketing and pushing out a poetry book, major outlets don't see it working, or in other words selling. Therefore, it takes somewhat of a brave soul to go ahead and release a book of poems. Some people told me that they are curious about how some poems managed to stick in their minds, even when they had forgotten about it.

My first intention with Mindful Motion was to write an epic novella in nothing but prose. I was convinced it would work, until I heard feedback from a few who listened and read my poetry. People tended to like the shorter poems that cut to the chase, rather than the longer versed prose that was given romantic treatment. One person stated that one of them hit me like a ton of bricks after [I heard it] a few months [later]. From a marketing perspective, I'm sure I'm guaranteed at least a few hundred sales of Ocean In the Drop.

I took on the constructive criticism and subsequently Ocean In The Drop was created. This is a collection of 100 poems on the subject of totality; oneness and the occupational hazards of separation.

Parcel From Kowloon (A Moving Meditation)

Our couched smartphones, they came from heroes,
Our friends from across the North Pacific,
What of those nets from outside those windows,
Are our first world problems horrific?
To hide some guilt let's mask solutions,
Argue a case of divine tragedy,
They don't care, those busy institutions,
Marketing and pushing their gadgetry,
Is it the hoi polloi that they implore?
The irony is the workers know more.

A Dynast Communiqué

Vectors of syntax move around ether,
And the clerks and merchants, all but many-
Few sow, so many try to be reaper,
Is it a wise pound or foolish penny?

A Peppermint Portmanteau

The peppermint box contains all the goods,
Some say it's a source of inspiration,
It is rare though, in my neck of the woods,
On good days, I go to a space station,
On other days, one feels square like blocks,
A pinch of flowers, wrapped in a bouquet,
So I have to thank the peppermint box,
A one of a kind organic buffet,
Together, removing all of life's locks.

Hare and the Tortoise

Some just want to see the whole wide world burn,
Like a slug filing for a tax return,
Slow pokes, forgiven for lack of concern,
A hare with a briefcase, too quick to earn,
The tortoise at the back too slow to learn,
But tortoise was tough, the tortoise was stern,
The hare was not and a chance he will spurn,
'Slow and steady', the lesson you learn.

Dear Metaphysics and Time

I felt shivers all over my body,
Shivers went all the way up my forehead,
Fingers, hands – cold, this is not a hobby,
And when you let go it's like breaking bread,
You eat what you need; it's there to serve you,
Everything else is very personal,
Some face demons, then made brand new,
Or at least if your perspective's internal,
Though that's nothing, for time is eternal.

Accessible Facts

Look…the bigger picture, what does it bring?
If it's hard to explain, it's not the truth,
The truth is easy; we are all one thing,
As every house has the need for a roof,
Women are queens and every man is king,
Look at the crowd if you ever need proof.

An Amicable Reverie

An act of kindness caught on camera,
An anchor reporting on what he just saw,
A large panda, hailed for his stamina,
Imagine if that was the rule of law…

Aude (Mystic Valley)

A bond that connects us, was all we knew,
I was indoors, outdoors - bloodshed grew,
My father protected me from the view,
Humbly he told me, I should leave the country,
To take the next plane and go somewhere sunny,
He said 'be a good girl, love yourself,
The best things are free, not from the shelf,
It's your story, not another's chapter,
Healing others was my main factor,
I then studied and became a doctor,
Settled down and gave birth to my daughter,
My homeland still under perpetual war,
Her beautiful land stripped down to the core,
Though, words in my head sing: Restore! Restore!
I know now, that God gave me a voice,
To reach those born with limited choice,
How do you breathe, let alone conquer fears,
With strength of character to hold back tears?
Truly life is suffering if I feel,
Even when I think, the pain is still real,
I can say that I have learnt two things,
The first is stillness and the calm it brings,
Like rain water in drought, quenching earth's thirst,
And the second is to always remember the first.

Augury (Tibet's Avocation)

Warmness of the heart, words from the lama,
Grains of sand positioned intricately,
Placing a vase around the mandala,
Harnessing peace metaphysically,
As layers are complete, the artists leave,
Allowing the wheel to turn its cycle,
Day two, the artist continues to weave,
Day three, the Kalachakra is final,
Now, a symbol to believe and achieve.

A Croupier's Avant-Garde Dilemma

What do we have here, charity – hedge fund,
Please don't click on that, they don't do combat,
I couldn't help it, it had to be done,
The union waits to collect their debt,
How many of them?
Hmm…about seven,
The average type, without a pot…
Tell them that their balance has been frozen,
That won't stop their aim,
Why? You'll be to blame,
No, do this before anyone has spoken,
What kind of charity are they really?
Stopping homelessness,
Pfftt…is this a test?
In the practical, but not in theory.

Matador and the Roaming Bull

Charging upwards, I was the roaming bull,
As if it were something from folklore,
She moved just in time, her thoughts were full,
What did you expect from a matador?
A female one at that, she was cunning,
The voice of reason, the voice of logic,
The mental dialogue that was running,
Expecting a clear mind in the tropic,
Commitment was what we were both shunning,
The roaming bull, charging, salut!
A beautiful detachment, adieu...

Mind Over Matter

I want new ideas, what's the solution?
Ether to ideas, what a transition!
Best ideas are the ones that flow freely,
Rigidity is found in a mausoleum,
Don't be stuck in thought thinking too deeply,

I don't get it, is your logic broken?
The trick is to stop thinking and then it's done,
Sit down on your chair and simply focus,
Remark how everything is contained in one,
Remove critters that plague the subconscious,

By all means, silence the mental chatter,
It has always been mind over matter.

Born to win

A knowing since birth,
That all souls are born to win,
Please enjoy the ride.

Orion's Belt

It takes time to develop good habits,
Bad ones usually multiply like rabbits,
Whenever bad thoughts pop up, I can it,
That peppermint box, it does help,
Jumping star systems to Orion's belt,
Name me some books like this on someone's shelf?
Can't stay too long though, got to go back down,
It leapt like a full stop chasing a noun,
This was bumblebee with the gold crown.

Arc

Had a convo' about cause and effect,
There's something about our feline friends,
Detachment is their specialist subject,
Hunting, caring, two of their many gems,
They always seem to have things in order,
It's like that even when things were tribal,
A trait they pass on to their daughter,
And humanity turns its full cycle,
A certain kind of unity en masse,
But how much longer does this circle last?

Divine Interlude

Is destiny a star alignment?
Do princes change their environment?
While others feed off scraps from the table,
Is goodness reserved for those who're able?
When cause meets effect, the law of Karma,
Working to and fro, the wheel of Dharma,
Circulating, keeping us from dismay,
Funny, sad, good and bad, life is a play,
House falls down, you get up and walk away.

Mothers

This is for you brave motherly figures,
Man never truly knows what mother's feel,
What of a female president – Maybe?
This moment in time, what do you see?
I see a woman hugging a baby,
Maternal instinct is reserved for she,
Parenting; a challenge that you relish,
You're the best, to those who keep down the drama,
So then, love your child and let them flourish,
That feeling you get when you're called mama!
The very best mothers remain unheard,
All kids say I have the best mum in the world.

Craft of Gratis

Modern day business for modern people,
A craft of gratis, defeats anything legal,
Applied ideas open up avenues,
To compete you need strong revenues,
The aim is not to be on the menu,
And if your aim is to provide true value,
Maintain it to an excellent standard,
If you can, make all questions answered,
Focus on good and goodness surfaces,
Stand your ground; believe in your services,
A firm grip of law and its specifics,
A bit like decoding hieroglyphics,
There isn't really an ideal game plan,
Or a number on its life span,
And if there was, it would be deceitful,
For the best things in life are free and simple.

Curtains Drawn

Curtain drawn, another action filled day,
London Turns to night, lamp posts flicker light,
Not a squeak is heard, roads are deserted,
And all of the traffic is diverted,
Still, all the other sirens alerted,
Underbelly groans of Boeing 747,
And it's just gone quarter past eleven,
Couples start to think of something witty,
Just Another day in London City,
The TVs switched on, the curtains are drawn.

Da Vinci

Guard Mona Lisa,
Simple adventure,
Water the driving force of all nature,
For lack of trying,
Felt it in the heart,
In Wilde's 'decay of lying',
The girl will still be smiling
The noblest pleasure is the joy of understanding
Art imitates life,
Life imitates art,
Knowledge has origins in our perceptions
Art is never finished, only abandoned,
Nothing is ever at random.

New Year's Eve

Clock shows ten hours until the New Year,
We must sober up, and keep the mind clear,
Saw something splashing, what's the commotion?
Eleven pulled down in the depths of the ocean,
Are we seeing right, or do our eyes deceive?
Subconscious elves, various serpents and Eve,
Then what does this dimension conceive?
Can we dance together, or is that plain naïve?
Forever swirling in the galaxy,
Coming back down after mind alchemy,
Now the wheel turns again, time starts anew,
This year, is the year of the break-through.

Sovereignty

How do you improve your ability?
Those times where you need space; sovereignty,
No judgement involved, to need space to grow,
Those who accomplish things carry a glow,
Positive energies they seem to emit,
The charge started when they chose to commit,
Whatever you're good at, improve on it,
So, spend minutes wisely, value your time,
And even if this is a line nine rhyme,
You have to repeat this from time to time.

Heart of Capital City

She terra-forms the garden once more,
Feeding breadcrumbs to the flock of pigeons,
In one great move, from the sky to the floor,
And the passer's by who were in legions,
Half of them ignored and half of them in awe,
The woman did work, only to withdraw,
Not discounting it was against the law.

Double-Dutch

What about the layers from old data?
Bad analysts look at the pro-rata,
Brushing off specs of dust from a fossil,
Discoveries can be quite colossal,
Even if it is I can't say too much,
A game we used keep playing called double-dutch.

Glass Pipe Frequency

Friend, don't take your brain for granted, use it!
Being right all the time is wrong,
Then you look at the current music,
Before you can play that new song,
Think of the records you bought,

Think Curtis Mayfield and Pink Floyd,
That kind of music can't be taught,
Analyse all you want, team Freud,
All this know how comes from void,
Character part of the tool-kit,
Don't take your brain for granted, use it!

E.f.f.e.c.t

Results are for show, effort is for real,
Whenever eating, focus on the meal;
Think of something to kick start the day,
And the effect is to do what you say,
In all of this reverie, life is the host,
The unlucky ones think they're the cause,
Then lucky for some, unlucky for most,
For Cause and Effect is made of divine laws.
Everything flows finely, eternal continues time -
That is an organism in design.

Treasure Chest (I Am)

Born in to this world, as blank as nothing,
Programmed by the senses into something,
A movable character, cast in flesh,
Breathing inspiration by air so fresh,
A controller of destiny for self,
But plans must be kept inside of your chest,
The dream that is kept inside of your chest,
Becomes very real without a moment's rest,
Before you find in you…life's treasure chest.

Hut Somewhere Made of Clay

There was no knowledge of language,
I wasn't one of the natives,
Of all places, a restaurant,
But of the highest echelon,
Can I order the special over here?
Translation garbled with fear,
Waiter, barely understood,
But understood the order for food,
Then my cultural attaché,
Phoned her protégé,
A violin student,
You never made recital?
You're usually quite prudent...
But now you've broken the cycle!
Sometime later, the phone was cut,
With signal gone in the hut,
A band called in to play the same day,
In a hut somewhere, made of clay.

Namaste

Travelling, you meet all sorts of people,
I was recommended to go to Nepal,
They say it teaches one to be peaceful,
Then I learned how to treat all equal,
And of all things good, how does it measure?
Compassion, love, kindness in gesture,
Be still and clam, patience is a virtue,
Both palms pressed together, pointing skyward,
Divine in me, salutes divine in you,
In kindness, Namaste is the byword.

Finding Memes

What's the deal with all these memes?
Living in a bubble like snot from phlegm,

Is making snap judgements all the rage?
Or, is this the way of the modern day sage?

Vote Now! Press the button with your finger,
You can be as famous as this singer,

Has the world gone insane?
Why not ask B. Wayne,
Put it on a meme and call me Bane.

Serenity

They say that silence is golden,
What of those who like to talk a good game?
That just leaves them out in the open,
Serenity is key and a calm frame,
After that, you accomplish what you've chosen.

Reticent Discourse

Why is it the best days are reticent?
The silent moments are most salient,
Everything seems to flow in harmony,
And moving away from conformity,
And to awareness, where it all happens,
That words won't cut it, only the actions,
Now bring yourself back to that quiet place,
If it takes some time, there's fear to displace.

Macrocosm Spore

I want to be a star, who do I follow?
Be the thing you think of, words are hollow,

But people stop me, like it's their mission,
Minimise speaking, so you can listen,

But why do I have to listen too?
Because everyone has a point of view,

And I know I've been wrong on few occasions,
But the thing about those equations,

If we're all one, then why are there wars?
...from under the microscope, we're all like spores.

Give Life to Your Dreams

Give life to your dreams,
Only you can make them grow,
Persistence, determination and passion,
Are the seeds to sow.
To make a dream become reality,
Is where success really lies,
With hard work, care and attention,
You can do it, but only if you try.
Look deep into your soul,
And make a positive life plan,
Whenever in doubt, 'stay focused',
Always remember, 'I can.'
Tomorrow's dream may never come,
Get busy today; there are lots more to be done,
Time is precious and not ours to keep,
Rewards are out there for yours to reap.

Opportunists Digest

Set out from the start, the motto was more,
For the umpteenth time, they've been frustrated,
Knocking on the opportunity door,
They kept knocking on the door and waited.
So the opportunists came to the fore,
Then they walked through the door they created.

Good Night's Sleep

I always do this when I'm tired,
Reflect on the day and think positive,
Read the chief aim before I get wired,
Hypnotic rhythm, its affirmative,
A good night's sleep and the paths it paves,
It sorts out the particles from the waves.

Another Gratitude Ode

Thank the heavens for this beautiful earth,
Spinning so carefree in the universe,
Power to create, thoughts that give birth
To words and numbers, to stanza and verse,
Thanks for awareness, the light we call home,
Delicate balance, formless and unknown,
Abundance of life and the way is shone
Thanks for energy for life and motions,
Guides us to and fro, to evolve and grow,
Change mind, change self, as above and so below,
Thanks for the wonderful Present Moment,
Live in the present, free mind, and ascend.

.

Humble's Play

Don't run before you can walk, try it first!
The fox drank the tea as it quenched its thirst,
No one cares if its unique, can it sell,
Neither of them, it's a story to tell,
I'm not really looking for a pay-day,
The fox then stood up and looked in dismay,
I don't need it, then the fox walked away,
Critics said that Humble's play was well versed,
The business fox looked back and feared the worst,
Don't run before you can walk, try it first!

Carpe Diem

Treat every second like it is holy,
With each passing minute, just still the mind,
Avail hours and build the day slowly,
As the mind motions, the world treats you kind,
Seize the day and use the moments boldly,
Make it a habit, do it all the time,
Go! Move forward, never say 'if only',
Movement backwards will only be a crime,
Ergo, Carpe Diem – always be growing!

Abstruse Simplicity

What can scare fire?
Is it more fire?
What will transpire?
When will it retire?
You want to conspire?
Go somewhere higher,
Take a bucket and conspire,
Fill and throw water,
That should scare fire.

Equanimity

I: A Great Place to Start

Wealth comes from the heart, a great place to start,
To believe in yourself and so with others,
To peace for peace and encourage lovers,
Find calmness, under pain body covers,
Inhale, exhale, and awaken fine sights,
Does the observer create days and nights?

II: Standing On the Shoulders of Giants

A symphony composed by Beethoven,
And celebration of sound was woven,
Da Vinci invented and sculpted art,
All great scholars, a muse through the heart,
Martin Luther King Jr. had a dream,
Now all rivers flow through a single stream,
Texts say Lao Tzu fled to the wilderness,
Left Tao Te Ching to cancel the bitterness,
Bruce Lee told the world to be like water,
Practicing until nights became shorter,
Muhammad Ali said I'm the greatest,
Making the heavyweight title his latest,
Float like a butterfly, sting like a bee,
Einstein's genius forced the world to see,
How everything is made of energy,
Socrates made the bold statement of nil,
To know that you know nothing is the pill,
Elegant natures, but built for the kill.

III: The Teacup Storm

No one said that life is easy,
Do work to make the pain vanish completely,
In times of strain, search yourself for courage,
Better yet, help others and encourage,
Render service into the world and smile,
Master your craft and go the extra mile,
The person who does this will always win,
Collectively, we make the whole world spin,
Understanding a universal truth,
By positively impacting the youth,
A message of dream, believe and achieve,
And compassion, give before you receive,
This should be taught in every single school,
And to top it off with the golden rule,
In any case, we should all be happy,
This can be a real possibility,
To live one vibrational energy.

IV: Calm after the Storm

Not to be with someone who makes you happy,
Be someone who makes you happy, the key,
Fruits of life, mature with age, like wine,
Self-love is the greatest love of all time,
Not that it can be depicted through rhyme,
To flow with waves that motion from the sea,
To fly so high and not get left behind,
To progress into domains, 'I' as 'we',
To feel from the heart and speak from the mind,
To act from depths within, two becomes three,
When the points meet, all actions are aligned,
The world opens up to you, then you see,
Leader of men, not following the blind,
Open heart, open eye, set your soul free,
With every sorrow, a silver cloud lined,
Consciousness elevates by degree,
The nature in which we are all designed,
Clear your mind, raise belief, flower the tree,
Of knowledge or life, which one do we find?
The choice is yours, how about love or glee?
Compassion has no limits, unconfined,
To find happiness, make others happy,
To live life: in equanimity.

Imperfectly Perfect

Certain frost in the air, fingertips numb,
And 149 million miles from the sun,

Gummy pavements and discarded food waste,
So much a far cry from a five star taste,

Now, bittersweet as the street sweeper sweeps,
Then purifies the earth, in bounds and leaps,

Vultures fly above, so warm and snugly
Derision, to find beauty in ugly,

Questions always asked, life is the subject,
Everything is perfectly imperfect.

A Bottled Message on the Sea Shore

The bottled message arrive in seas mild,
Knowledge, wisdom, understanding compiled
With Tao written, Lao Tzu fled to the wild
The premise was simple, be like a child,
To have a childlike spirit, not childish,
With a definite purpose, not a wish,
Wisdom can be found in the Tao,
There is nothing to gain, or to ask how,
Understanding is in the here and now,
Eternal brightness from the stars above,
Is this what our universe is proud of?
Alone in thought, but together in love,
United we stand, divided we fall,
Lift your consciousness and break down the wall,
Educe what is inside you, great and small
Some people understand better through sharp pain,
Some understand the sun when it rains,
One thing remains which universe retains,
Infinite energy pervades domains,
With absence of thought, see us all as one,
Take this message and our Dynasties' done.
It is better this way in the long run,
Listen to those folks that live in Nepal.
Understanding, you were born with it all.

Knowledgeable Ramblings of Wise Folk

The lust for power, the lust for greed,
Are us beings right to live by this creed?
In a bamboo shack, the wise man speaks,
Be humble my friend, can you heed?
Life is but a journey,
So take what you need,
While the book keeps burning
The page keeps turning;
Leaders read,
And readers lead.

Less Is More

Less is always more,
Possessing things adds sorrow,
Be free and let go.

Life Game

Here, the game of life,
Commitment, desire,
Strong will, and prepared,
Willing to take risks,
Can you brave failure?
Days without results,
Months of drudgery,
And years of planning,
Setbacks will occur,
What about loved ones?
Love yourself firstly,
You are the loved one,
Trust your own instincts,
And labour with your love,
What about money?
Think of it like this,
To gain affluence
Provide good service,
Use the golden rule,
Do I deserve this?
A sapling either,
Growing or dying,
You were given all,
Through the highs and lows,
The universe flows,
How do I prevail?
Belief is vital,
Master the basics,
Don't ever look back,
And all will be fine…

Giggling Buddha

Sunrise, Sunset, loyalty and Trust,
Building an empire was always a must,
Sarcasm eroded with dust,
Just like a sports car bent with rust
Hope and progress underneath stress,
Clean heart under your vest,
Dance the best, until spirit rests,
How many persons have run this race?
How many souls will take my place?
Do you know the person behind this face?
Sitting cross legged under the Bodhi tree,
His heart sings, filled with glee,
I'm you and you're me,
Laughing ad-infinitum,
Hilarious ultimatum,
The way was not the sky,
But the way was in the heart.

Focus: A Comedian's Reprise

So full of self-belief,
Not a need for external relief,
Banish failure and embarrassment,
Like quantum entanglement,
Unlock the key,
An open heart, maybe,
Life seemed indefinite,
Purpose far too definite,
Jug fills drop by drop,
Rain falls drip by drip,
Progress, inch by inch,
Forget the past,
Though you learn from it,
Not outcome dependant,
Capture this moment,
Don't look back,
Don't even look forward,
Focus on now,
Never the how,
Slow and tedious,
The art of presence,
Altogether,
One with the Universe,
But now your heart is oh so strong,
For heart is where the home belongs.

Show and Prove

Every time I've talked about it,
I've never quite got it,
Mouths should be closed, I admit,
The price you pay when you commit,
This leaves room to show and prove it.

Mindful Motion I

To find a cure for the dying seagulls,
Some just ran, some died down, rhythmic lulls,
Touching the land, where there are broken skulls,
It motioned with the water with packed hulls,
The echoes of the distant ship felt base,
Past the morning sun, to see open space,
Lined up one by one, ready to race,
Though, plentiful is the aqua harvest,
It is not who's the hardest, but the smartest,
Cries of trying to save the manatees,
Yield lucre, justified insanity,
An evolving sphere of humanity,
Feel the radiance from the galaxy,
Capturing the essence of what's inside,
Educing genius, a mental ride,
How can one box in, something that's so wide,
A strange paradox, to add and divide,
Play is our work, and work is our bride,
A theme, that resonates across worldwide.

Mindful Motion II

Simply just commit,
Never, ever quit,
Stop fighting with it,
Be aligned with it,

You're a contender,
Be and know yourself,
Let world surrender,
And then you break through
Create something new,
Life simply helps you,

Simple art reader,
Look in the mirror,
Be your own leader,
Follow your own heart,
To master your craft

Flow with the ocean,
A simple notion,
To work and play in,
A mindful motion.

Suburbia Sunshine

Britain's eyes are glazed, gazing through the double
glaze,
Gloriously giggling at the Gregorian maze,
Is it a delusion to think we are living happy days?
Forever asking the boss for a raise,
Or is it just another part of this Khali-Yug stage?
Of sheep and wolves, who has the better appraise,
Writing essays in the dark for which it portrays,
Looking for grays at night, with their dodgy ways,
We have no time to fill these cheap surveys,
Britain's eyes are glazed,
Gazing through the double glaze.

Tropic Sunshine

Pineapple seasoned with salt and chilli,
All I needed in this beach, no – really!
Then it started to rain, storms were brewing,
In the sky, I could see what the clouds were chewing,
There we were, hidden under umbrellas,
All the women, hugging their fellas,
Were we here on the right or wrong day?
Locals busy chatting, they know it's a play,
The pineapple vendor still sells his wares,
And the locals buying, paying their fares,
I look around and its visitor's fear,
There's been worse weather; this one's nowhere near,
All of a sudden, we hear a big cheer,
Song and dance at the corner of my eye,
We all looked on, as the rain said goodbye.

Mother Nature's Light

You stand for much, your words shine with light,
Is it a thousand hands or thousand eyes?
After a while, I can tell that you're right,
Working from heaven's open skies,
In my lifespan, likely I won't fully understand,
How could God play this miraculous hand.
Mother Nature's light, shining in the night.

Mount Choisy

Shovelling sands that grip the sun's rays,
Peering in the clouds arrests the dark days,
Sunset paradise, heaven enchanted,
Humans can never take this for granted,
Flooded, in rise and fall of tides long gone,
Come racing back again, where it belongs,
Bot flies swish upon specs of stratosphere,
And here, is a mountain measured in fear,
To climb it, stray from the path of failure,
Crashing waves becomes hefty harmony,
This wonder renders certain agony,
Twinkling unknown of unspoilt billows,
Gateway to subconscious, open windows,
Working day and night, the view was unveiled
Just after two nights, the mountain was scaled.

Mr. Fox Man I

Mr. Fox man, in your business attire,
Holding the umbrella in the sun, 'till you retire,
We shook hands once, whatever did we conspire?
Was it to pillage the earth, or something much higher?
The bread does break, and poor countries left dire,
We have no time to wallow in the mire,
Forever in meet with the seller and the buyer,
Can we un-light this burning desire?
Mr. Fox man, immortally in your business attire.

Mr. Fox Man II (Reprise)

Above those hills, look! A pot of gold,
Ascending over the land, until you turn old,
Repining restlessness, so very uncontrolled,
It couldn't be shared, for it was oversold,
It never was read, for it was always foretold,
Mr. Fox man came back,
This time with fool's gold.

Abundance

Peace is found within, don't seek it without,
Inner peace of self, you bring the best out,
Be nice to people, it can bring good health,
For opinions intangible,
All knowledge is formational,
Up and down, moods somewhat transitional,
Pain is there, Suffering is optional,
The truth is, love is unconditional
Silent, keen and alert in the moment,
What it is, nothing's ever accident,
The Shapeless, nameless, Boundless and formless,
Insight after insight, no need to try,
It comes from the heart and not from the sky,
Depth needs height, Dark needs light
Like attracts like,
Through all valley and peaks
The wholeness speaks,
Break mind made ceilings
Practice mindfulness
We Are Beings, Not Doings
Be open not needy, Be happy and healthy,
Be rich and wealthy,
Love yourself,
Love everybody,
Clarity of mind and vision,
Universe speaks and student listens,
As a rule of thumb,
What you think you become.

No Limit

Entertainments that help the world spin,
Two sides battle it out, right vs. left,
Pick your side, now…which is going to win,
And for the side that wins are they most blessed?
Whether it be violent or non-violent,
There is still a competitive spirit,
What would happen if everything's silent?
I guess you could life with no limit.

Parlance (Victimless)

No more the victim with its ragged claws,
Pointing the finger and clutching on straws,
Victim mentality-
A masterpiece for the blind,
For everyone else, fantasy in kind.

A Lucky Coin from a Bird's Eye View

Bird's eye view of a microchip society,
Human traffic flowing through veins electronically,
Buildings imitate some sort of circuitry,
What exactly is it powering?
Is it widening or narrowing?
And we keep expanding,
Not satisfied with a moon landings,
What remains of the centre of the earth?
Or have we known that ever since birth…

One Step Closer

Fear; the gargoyle that often clouds one's view,
Stare down the worst thing that happened to you,
And turn it into a harmless story,
So now you're one step closer to glory.

The Zen Monkey

The monkey meditates in silence,
Luminous being, as bright as the sun,
Nothing distracted him, even a siren,
After a while, he finally reached the one,
In line with truths, but flowing like water,
To do it, balance out the equation,
So change your life and the world will alter,
He never spoke after that occasion.

Can We Take This Dream? (Home)

Night falls and touches the swaying ocean,
The green leaves fall from the coconut trees,
Whistling people, all in full motion,
The fire pit burns with sail caught marlin,
Female cook, with the humour of Carlin,
A wry smile, she turns the roasted lobster,
Ginger dipping sauce, a complete roster,
We all have fun, feeling like young Bourdains,
Pointing skyward, we hope it never rains,
Tucking into nature in its essence,
The sky, sea and sand in phosphorescence,
Stars are clear, heavens in luminescence,
No ATMs, internet, no calls home,
Feels so good and if all roads lead to Rome,
Then we ask, why can't we take this dream home?

Plastic Promulgation

It is a journey, but we did arrive,
After a long three hour, four wheeled drive,
We stopped to get fast food by the beach,
At the drive through:
We made our food speech.
Only in here where you forget price tags,
Passively accepting the plastic bags,
The view outside the car was the ocean,
Blue crystal waves moving in one motion,
Before anyone could throw the plastic,
One of us saw something drastic,
He looked at us all and made a decree-
It's the cause of poison in the sea!
We looked with contempt at this human feed,
That sudden insight, most of us agreed,
I wonder; should we all live by this creed?

Poetic Justice

There we are, all well versed,
Clean cut, with no exclamation marks!
Kicking footballs into the vowels parks,
Stanzas upon stanzas of question marks,
We have to read the book, to see where the story arcs,
It didn't end with any sort of peace,
For we were kicked out by the grammar police.
And with every pun, we still had fun,
This prose never promoted any toughness,
Simply 'cause it was poetic justice.

Present War

Emperor unimpressed,
Sought a general,
General unimpressed,
Humility of the heart,
Sought out soldiers,
Happy to part
With few broken hearts
And some broken carts,
A Village lay to rest,
The Emperor so blessed,
That he passed the test,
General started muttering,
Soldiers started stuttering,
Much pain and suffering,
Bird started fluttering,
All Weapons blunted
And all money spent,
Heavens' letter quickly sent,
Now, to end this rift:
Today is the gift,
And it is the present.

Red and Blue

Fire? The message wasn't delivered,
It gave courage, but then bewildered,
What then of the mind stuff, is it useful?
What, the motion part? Yes, if mindful,
If not, then it will go over your head,
So learn it, then a message you'll embed,
To truly know, put it into practice,
So then value your time, perfect tactics,
Like composing a musical score,
It is a case of doing more and more,
With less and less, but always improving,
The answer is in showing and proving.

Robotic Paint

Knowing less about anthropology,
Technology – grows faster and faster,
And wired wireless technology,
Data, on the walls it seems to plaster,
What are these machines trying to master?
Information at the touch of a pad,
Resources aplenty, across worldwide,
Then does that mean we should all be glad?
We want TV, get a satellite dish,
All kinds of entertainment that we wish,
We want more articles, we want it now,
Checking on the NASDAQ and the Jones Dow,
A necessity to push the products,
The need to fill the stomach,
The fast food shops are here to stay,
Unless organic keeps them at bay,
Ordering food with online currency,
Delivered to our doors hurriedly,
Maximum capacity, buy your car,
Fill it up with petrol, then get far,
Production line moves faster than the eye,
No human error, computers don't cry,
The social hub, the chitter, the chatter,
Asleep or awake, are you the latter?

Routine Wake-Up

I tell myself this again and again,
When all is against you, apply yourself,
And all those lessons? Master your own self,
I mean lessons in life, not the book shelf,
If you focus on the task, concentrate;
Make things easier and don't complicate.

Sanctuary

After relaxation, out comes the new
Everybody has their sanctuary,
Even the misinformed and misled too,
Equal amounts of peace actually,
But why do they go back to the grindstone?
So then I realised all of a sudden,
There are bills to pay; they must buy their home,
It must be some kind of reset button.

Sapphire

An ecstatic motion, and now the sky,
Hugging the planet with her watchful eye,
Myriad celestial stars lay to bare,
Questioning the cosmos below her stare,
Locked in the present, now, not there or where,
Mystic energy and dreams do pervade,
Lives on forever, no need to persuade
Feeling so small, panting, breaths in the chest,
Quiet and still, eternally reflects,
Celestial objects, Give life to fire,
Heaven sent then sapphire was conspired.

Zen, when – Now!

When do we reach Zen?
Caught beneath the red dragon's breath,
A clear acceptance of birth and death.

When do we reach Zen?
Battering away the drums of the past,
Leave future behind, it will never last.

When do we reach Zen?
Not a care in the world, living it free,
Blossoming like petals from the peach tree.

When do we reach Zen?
Happiness comes from the heart,
Humanity whole in its part.

When do we reach Zen?
Focused on the why,
Disregarding how.
When do we reach Zen?
This moment called now!

The Unnameable Poem

Silently filling the moment of now,
Vast introspection, in the here and now,
What is this majestic force that pervades?
There's nothing so large, there's nothing so vast,
The mind likes to wander into the past,
Gallops to the future, so very fast,
Finally, the here and now, long at last
Be like the water, and empty your mind,
If not cared for, it can never settle,
Cold and rigid and can sting like nettle,
Water properly, with tranquillity,
Harness power of positivity,
Opens to door to new possibility,
Once the mind is reclaimed, Suffering stops
One thing remains, The Tao cannot be named.

Best Day

I arrived with some time to stand and stare,
Approaching to the man in the mirror,
I lived life today with a mind so clear,
Why be over there, when you can be right here,
Listen with your body, sing and cheer,
Enlightenment can feel so very near,
To feel with the heart, all you've ever wanted,
Silence the mind, and be free from 'content',
The grass is always green in the moment,
The canvas of life, so enchanted,
The heart vibrations make a wish granted,
You are the universe manifested,
Reap what you sow, the cosmic harvest,
In stillness, each second feels infinite,
Spacious, free, fleeting, but magnificent,
Touching something so unknown and wordless,
But, yet - feeling nothing, like it's formless,
External forces are merely harmless,
We're all connected as one, regardless,
Being present is a truth you harness,
Every now and then, the mind does wonder,
Staying in the present is the answer,
A life spent this way, is one of honour,
To read this again, a silent encore,
To play in this life of formless contour,
Today is the best day I've had, for sure.

A Silent Epiphany

Is there time to rest?
Yearning for the best,
Balancing the checks,
Minds settle for less,
Find the key and door,
Eagle tries to soar,
Answer: less is more,
Hope the stars align,
The Bane of mankind,
The desiring mind,
Go beyond and find,
That there is no past,
Because it won't last,
There is no future,
Just something called,
The present adventure,
It came back and said,
The Eagle ain't dead,
The Prey was misled,
All noise is absent.
Only the Present,
Change is forever,
In a silent epiphany,
A Mystery, like the eternal Tao,
The master asks why, not wondering how,
Silently aware,
In The Here and now.

Departure At 8 O' Clock

Stomach turns as I check in the airport,
Head checks for my ticket and passport,
Illusory feeling of peace and comfort,
Depart the land like packages in export,
I seek voyage to this remote resort,
finding happiness outside, dreams distort
Forever seeking a queen's consort,
Abort the mission, and thwart what holds true,
Cut short the audition,
Forever surrounded by skies of blue…

Submerged

Champagne padlock, fuzzy little beings,
Tykes, the lot of them all having fun,
And they want you to collect their winnings,
But funny, you can't grab hold of the sun.
Fold it up. Put it in your pocket,
It is the very thing they judge you for,
Truth's free, that's why lies are on the market,
Those who are awakened, a lie is a bore,
Who's to say that flowers are illegal,
Is it but an instrument of them too,
A justified crime, for being regal?
But a round of applause for those mind mass,
I don't have the answers, no one has,
Yes, that something where the well to do joins,
Those fuzzy little beings just want your coins.

Sun In Sight

Today I was going to read a book,
I just had breakfast, so no need to cook,
Go to the mirror and get a quick look,
'Always willing to learn, and accept change',
With a drink in hand, and the beach in range,
Sways in the tropic wind, sand and sea twinned,
Line between life and dreams so gently thinned,
Mind clear from tide, clarity for the eye,
Tranquil supported by the hammock's net,
Counting the moments for the sun to set,
Sipping tea, hammock holds, sturdy and tight,
Hovering slightly, a comfortable height,
I said I would read, but now I will write,
The body relaxed, sleeping through the night.

A Tale from the Glacial Age

That was the last time I asked for time,
There, stood still, in frozen peninsula,
Lost in a blizzard of snow, snow sublime,
What if thought is tracked by the nebula?
But then I would have found my way back home,
A cautionary tale from travels long gone,
Do we know it all, in a cocooned dome?
Now, instinct kicks in and the path is shown,
A while to realise that it's not all mine,
That was the time I asked for the time.

Hunter Gatherer, Reacting on Instinct

People flock to see this specimen,
Certain effect, digested in the abdomen,
Only way to find it,
To be in the moment,
It will be gone, if too greedy
So you mustn't be too needy,
Who's the manufacturer?
Is it the Hunter-gatherer
Reacting on instinct,
A biological imprint,
In the wild, are things really better?
Like being inside to hide from the weather?
Such is the case; we like to box it in,
Deep down, the truth is nature always wins,
Reason why, we have so many kings,
Sand castle, built with a few grains,
Moat around it is what remains,
Not decided on who takes the reign,
Inside the castle,
A particular parcel
Lay a mushroom,
In the master bedroom
Amanita Something-scaria,
Then I remembered the hysteria,
Be in the present. The only area.

Three Birds That Flew Away From San Fernando

15 minutes from that cosy condo
Sitting by the beach of San Fernando,
Brushing crumbs from a bread and butter sarnie,
Staring at the barracks of the old Spanish army
Then a brightly coloured bird flew right on the shoulder,
Another sang the song of beauties' beholder,
With a blue-ish coat, another bird pecked some lunch,
Without the trappings of a credit crunch,
To capture this moment,
Was a hunch?
But they flew away,
Leaving it absent,
In quiet contemplation,
What in God's creation?
The three birds that flew away,
Still pondered to this day.

Timeless

Tick-Tock, Tick-Tock,
What happens, between those tocks?
Does time stand still, between sand and rocks,
Does it hold the key to all of life's locks?
Time waits for no one, who doesn't listen,
The now, a diamond that so brightly glistens,
So eternal in its rhythm,
It can't be held, paints an infinite scene
Never compelled, you feel it in the sky,
You see it in your eye,
But it cannot be seen,
Cannot be caught,
lays between, gaps in thought.

Siren

They saw you in dreams,
Saw lust, it brightly gleamed,
So very true it seemed,
Bought a return ticket,
For this soul, did it redeem?
The hustle was large;
Although it was clean,
But they were bluffing,
Only to be left with nothing,
Organic thoughts, led to a broken path,
In the end, who had the last laugh?

Beach

Boundless borders,
Endless waters,
Adventurous yachters,
Charismatic plotters,
Horizon spotters.

HMRC Romance

If it weren't for the bankers after my back,
Or the Goblin merchants after my stack,
My pound of flesh would have been rotted,
Like a broken pen, wet and blotted,
How many like me has HMRC plotted?
Out of this earth like a NASA rocket,
But in this hustle, who am I to knock it?

Vibrational Values

We carefully sip the goblet of wine,
From dusk to dawn, always thinking what's mine,
I ask to read a book without a spine,
And to worship a God that is divine,
Brevity loves the simplest of rhyme,
Onwards and upwards and without decline,
Clocks will count the seconds as full of time,
The road to success, is a heavy climb,
Not using one's mind, can be such a crime,
Use it properly and it's so sublime.

Empty Boat

How we adore the moment, when stillness speaks,
Empty boat left stranded by coral reef,
Nothing around it, but something beneath,
Suppressed memories of something so deep,
Is man awake or wide asleep?
And is this why the world sometimes weeps?
Are we all farmers sowing just to reap?
Or is the empty boat a shepherd,
That leads and I am the sheep?
All I do is laugh and enjoy life's peaks,
How we adore the moment, when stillness speaks.

Watch over the fire

When the flame is big,
Please, pour some water on it,
Cause and effect, done.

We Did It All In The Name Of... (Inspired By George Orwell's Animal Farm)

Mowing grass by the ton,
We did it all in the name of fun,
Making fun of the thin blue line,
We did it all in the name of fun,
At first we did it to get very rich,
And we worked and worked until we got zilch,
We did it all in the name of fun,
Trigger happy, and off the rockers,
Double whammies stuffed in their lockers,
They did it all in the summer of love,
Kindling missus and flying doves,
They got so high; touching planes above,
They did it all in the name of fun,
Then oinkees raised the price,
After that we stopped being so nice.
That too was done in the name of fun.

What Is

What is life without a dream?
What is a plan, without a scheme?
What is a smile without a gleam?
What is a wave, without a stream?
What is day sans carpe diem?
What is self without self-esteem?
What is a scare without a scream?
What is anthem without a theme?
What is discipline without regime?
What is a player without a team?
What is the truth, without justice?
Or what if, what is simply is.

Wind out of Sails

It is the simple game of sink or swim,
Some can't paddle, so the result is grim,
It's all in the water, drowning aside,
And it makes everything else seem worthwhile,
It's the driving force that livens the day,
And water is the closest to the way.

X For Expressions

What is this substance, which dreams are made of?
Is it the DMT from R.E.M?
And what is the essence from which it stems?
I sleep and close my eyes and feel life's gems,
Is it time to go yet, I only ask when,
Then a voice said write, for life is your pen...
Trusting the wisdom of sages, simply,
Turn all your dreams into reality,
But, how do I use this dreaming substance?
Think wealth and receive wealth in abundance,
Learn to live life without regrets, and shine,
Learn to move forwards in times of decline,
Be here and now, lose the concept of time,
To reach for everything in the black hole,
Can one extract a particle of soul?
Can another person share the world whole?
Can artistic merit beat price control?
Carrying out life from the Dead Sea scroll,
Expressing yourself truly is life's goal,
The nexus of time and space is right here,
Create your own roads how, no need to fear,
Speed ahead; there is no final frontier,
Make living your one and only career,
The universe will give you the all clear,
And all you fears and doubt will disappear,
Do your work and others will admire,
Life is a movie, make it your premiere.

Youthful Vigour

The clock approaches midnight, sky turns black,
Moon hangs high, its commemorative plaque,
Gleaming above the cries of the wolf pack,
What possible message can we take back?
That it's safe to live in a wooden shack,
Or pursue higher goals to 'stay on track'?
To face your fears and demons, then attack?
They say clarity of vision aids you,
To see us as one from a worldly view,
We're told as kids to keep dreams and pursue,
Then is youthful vigour the real breakthrough?
The older we get, the more we construe,
The younger we get, the more we renew,
Keep youthful vigour and never subdue.

Personal Buddha

Party started, everyone felt cadence,
All inhibitions went out of windows,
Then, everyone forgot about agents,
Is it Buddha; 50 friends, 50 woes?
That's why there are lonely thrones,
And why you're meant to be happy on your own!

Mindful Motion: Ocean In The Drop

What is it that makes water so special?
Because it can fill up any vessel?
Through all its powers, it affects most on earth,
It's the first thing that breaks during birth,
Said to be the closest thing to the way,
It can't tell between prey and the word pray,
Water represents many other things,
Power, subconscious and motion it brings,
To quote a legendary music vet-
Some people feel the rain, others get wet,
Water is powerful, yet can submit,
No one this planet can live without it,
There is a flipside to this element,
The poor of this world beg for a droplet,
Think of those in need, where the climates hotter,
Who have no access to clean drinking water,
So, is the glass half full or half empty?
Be grateful, drink it, in our world there's plenty.

Tao Of I Am

All I can produce is a how to guide,
So then, the why and what is up to you,
There are many methods, tried and untried,
I have many my ways that helped me breakthrough,
What I can say is find a way how,
Find the right balance and make it your Tao.

A Good Deed

Some people see red, some people see blue,
Some other people see shades of what's true,
But with all respect, why do I have a choice?
Why is there silence, when I have a voice?
Another dichotomy of life's split,
How many more good deeds can we commit?

Source

Peeling through layers of humanity,
And everything that ends in anity,
What's left after all of the travelling?
A spectrum of dancing lights gathering,
A wonderful life to be mastering,
After all things said and done,
How do we stay with the source of one?

Sphere

A day has started from a circle's spin,
The celebrated harness from within,
Everything that is and has ever been,
So we end the story, where we begin.

Additional Notes

The best pieces of poetry I have ever written have always come to me easily and fast. Messages are important to have in poems. However, sometimes what can be as important is the motive behind writing the poems. While I do like to leave my poetry open to interpretation, here are some additional notes on a few of them.

1. Hare And The Tortoise – this chronicles the classic fable of the hare and the tortoise. The message here was learnt from excessively living like the hare. The importance of looking at the bigger picture and keeping calm and steady is cited, because in the end the tortoise like qualities always wins.

   Written in London, 2014.

2. Accessible Facts – I wrote this one to symbolise how similar everyone is regardless of our differences. I initially wanted to express how anyone who treats their mother like a queen would be raised as a king or queen. That message is elaborated in the poem Mothers.

   Written in London, 2014.

3. <u>Finding Memes</u> – I used to browse through social media and take it seriously until something made me rethink its effectiveness. It was meme culture. To those of you who don't know what one is, it is usually an image with a caption expressing a certain viewpoint or a collectivised opinion. I don't mind them, as long as they possess usefulness!

Written in Paris, 2012.

4. <u>Equanimity</u> – if you were to ask me which is one of my favourite poems of my own, I would say this one is. It is by far the longest one in the book. I've also named dropped a few figures throughout history that have amazed the world. I know that they have amazed me enough to include them in a poem. Equanimity points to the path of achievement, particularly in the western world and cites the importance of possessing a clear mind.

Written in London, 2012.

5. <u>Mont Choisy</u> – This isn't based on a mountain called Choisy, but a place along a tropical beach. I remember it being so peaceful and tranquil, a few people were there. A few friends and I were singing songs around a fire next to the sun set by the beach. We talked candidly to each other and on that day a few people overcame their fears to boot. It was a memorable occasion that stuck in my mind.

Written in Grande-Baie, 2010.

Lightning Source UK Ltd.
Milton Keynes UK
UKOW04f2114300414

230900UK00016B/633/P